D1622662

HOMEMADE CHRISTMAS

Holiday SNACKS & APPETIZERS

Gail Sattler

BARBOUR
PUBLISHING

© 2002 by Barbour Publishing, Inc.

ISBN 1-59310-038-8

All rights reserved. No part of this publication may be reproduced or transmitted in any form or by any means without written permission of the publisher.

Cover image © Corbis

All Scripture quotations are taken from the HOLY BIBLE, NEW INTERNATIONAL VERSION®. NIV®. Copyright © 1973, 1978, 1984 by International Bible Society. Used by permission of Zondervan Publishing House. All rights reserved.

Published by Barbour Publishing, Inc., P.O. Box 719, Uhrichsville, Ohio 44683, www.barbourbooks.com

Member of the
Evangelical Christian
Publishers Association

Printed in Italy.
5 4 3 2 1

Contents

"Today in the town of David
a Savior has been born to you;
he is Christ the Lord.
This will be a sign to you:
You will find a baby
wrapped in cloths
and lying in a manger."

LUKE 2:11–12

Christmas is a tremendous time of joy,
and there is no better way to celebrate than to
share this time with friends and loved ones.
Our Lord calls us to fellowship together,
so let us do that by sharing our homes
and our friendship, and add to the fun
with some good food to share.
May the joy of the Christmas season be with you
this holiday and at all times.

*"He has shown kindness by giving you
rain from heaven and crops in their seasons;
he provides you with plenty of food
and fills your hearts with joy."*

ACTS 14:17

Appetizers

*My soul will be satisfied
as with the richest of foods;
with singing lips my mouth will praise you.*

PSALM 63:5

Sweet and Sour Pork Appetizers

1 lb ground cooked ham
1 lb ground pork
2 c bread crumbs

1 c milk
2 eggs, beaten
1 tsp salt

Mix and shape into meatballs.

SAUCE:

1½ c brown sugar
¾ c vinegar

¾ c water
1 tsp dry mustard

Pour sauce over meatballs and bake uncovered at 325° for 40 minutes.

Sour-Sweet Wiener Tidbits

1 c currant jelly
1 lb wieners or cocktail sausages

¾ c prepared mustard

Combine mustard and jelly in top of double boiler; heat. Add bite-sized wieners; heat thoroughly.

Mini Meat Pies

Tart shells, baked

FILLING:

1 lb ground veal or beef
1 lb ground pork
1 can cream of mushroom soup

1 medium onion, chopped
Salt, pepper, garlic to taste
Butter

Sauté onions in butter, add meat, and cook until meat loses color. Add spices and soup. Cool filling before using.

Microwave Mozza-Mushrooms

4 slices bacon, cooked and
  crumbled
12 medium fresh mushroom caps

12 cubes of mozzarella cheese
Grated Parmesan cheese

Place equal amounts of crumbled bacon into each cap. Top with cheese cube. Place on microwave tray or glass dish. Microwave on high for about a minute or until cheese melts. Sprinkle with Parmesan cheese and serve.

Honey-Glazed Chicken Wings

3 lb chicken wings
⅓ c soy sauce
2 tbsp oil
2 tbsp chili sauce (or ketchup
   or barbecue sauce)
¼ c honey

1 tsp salt
½ tsp ground ginger
¼ tsp garlic powder (or 1
   clove garlic, minced)
¼ tsp cayenne pepper

Separate wings at joints. Mix remaining ingredients. Pour on chicken. Cover and refrigerate, turning chicken occasionally, at least one hour or overnight.

Heat oven to 375°. Drain chicken, reserving marinade. Place chicken on rack in foil-lined broiler pan. Bake 30 minutes. Brush chicken with reserved marinade. Turn chicken and bake for another 30 minutes or until tender.

Herb and Cheese-Filled Cherry Tomatoes

1 (4-oz) pkg cream cheese, softened
½ tsp dried dill weed

1 tsp milk
15–16 cherry tomatoes

Combine cream cheese, dill, and milk until blended. Remove top and seeds from tomatoes. Drain tomatoes upside down on paper towel for a few minutes. Fill with cream cheese mixture. Chill or serve immediately.

Pita Bites

1 bag pitas, halved and cut into triangles, or minisized pitas
1 c mayonnaise
1 onion, chopped

½ c slivered almonds
½ lb cheddar cheese
6 slices crumbled cooked bacon

Combine everything except pitas. Spread mixture on top of pitas. Cook at 400° for 8–10 minutes.

Guacamole Bites

2 cans refrigerated crescent
    dinner rolls
$\frac{1}{2}$ tsp cumin
$\frac{1}{2}$ tsp chili powder
1 container ($1\frac{1}{2}$ c) guacamole
    or 3 ripe mashed avocados

1 (8-oz) pkg cream
    cheese
1 tomato, chopped
$\frac{1}{4}$ c bacon bits
$\frac{1}{4}$ c sliced ripe olives

Separate crescent rolls into long rectangles, place on un-greased cookie sheet, and press over bottom of pan. Sprinkle with cumin and chili, bake for 17 minutes at 375° or until golden brown. Cool.

Combine guacamole and cream cheese until smooth, spread over crust, and chill. Top with remaining ingredients.

Makes 60.

Cheesy Mushroom Rounds

2 (8-oz) tubes refrigerated
  crescent rolls
2 (8-oz) pkg cream cheese,
  softened
3 (4-oz) cans mushroom
  stems and pieces, drained
  and chopped

1¼ tsp garlic powder
½ tsp Cajun seasoning
1 egg
1 tbsp water
2 tbsp grated Parmesan
  cheese

Unroll crescent dough into 2 long rectangles; seal seams and perforations.

Combine cream cheese, mushrooms, garlic powder, and Cajun seasoning. Spread over dough to within 1 inch of edges. Roll jelly-roll style and seal edges and place seam-side down on a greased baking sheet.

Beat egg and water, brush over roll, and sprinkle with cheese.

Bake at 375° for 20–25 minutes or until golden brown. Cut into slices. Makes 16.

Mushroom Nappies

(can be made ahead and frozen)

3 tbsp butter or hard margarine
1 c onion, chopped
2 c fresh mushrooms, chopped
1 c grated mozzarella cheese
1/4 c grated Parmesan cheese
1 tsp parsley flakes
1 large egg

1/2 tsp whole oregano
Salt
12 slices white bread
1/3 c butter or hard
   margarine, softened
3 yellow cheese slices

Beat egg, chop butter into chunks with a fork and add to egg, then stir in onion, mushrooms, cheeses, parsley, oregano, and salt. Set aside.

Cut off crusts from bread slices. Roll each slice lightly with rolling pin to flatten. Butter slices. Cut each slice into 4 squares. Press, buttered side up, into tiny muffin tins. Fill with mushroom mixture using about 1 1/2 teaspoons for each one.

Cut each cheese slice into 16 small squares. Put 1 square on top of each tart. Bake in 350° oven for 20–25 minutes. Makes 4 dozen.

Crab Wonton

(freezes well)

3 tbsp cornstarch
1 (8-oz) pkg cream cheese, softened
1 (8-oz) can crabmeat, drained
½ tsp Accent seasoning

2 tbsp green onion, minced, including some tops
1 (1-lb) pkg wonton wrappers (about 60)

Lightly dust waxed paper with cornstarch and set aside. Cream cream cheese; blend in crab, Accent, and onions. Place ¾ teaspoon in center of each wonton piece. Moisten the edges with water then fold into a triangle. Press edges to seal. Fry a few at a time in vegetable oil at 365° until golden. Turn once. Drain; serve. Makes 5 dozen.

Crab-Stuffed Mushrooms

1 lb mushrooms
1 (6-oz) tin crabmeat
1 egg, well beaten
$\frac{1}{4}$ c fine bread crumbs
$\frac{1}{4}$ c tomato juice
1 tsp lemon juice
Dash Tabasco

1 tsp onion, finely
  chopped
2 tsp celery, finely
  chopped
$\frac{1}{2}$ tsp salt
$\frac{1}{2}$ c bread crumbs
$\frac{1}{4}$ c melted butter or
  margarine

Mix first 9 ingredients and fill mushroom caps. Toss remaining bread crumbs with melted butter and sprinkle over filled caps. Brown 6 inches from heat 5–8 minutes, or bake in 350° oven 15–20 minutes.

Tiny Ham-Stuffed Tomatoes

1 pt cherry tomatoes
1 (4$\frac{1}{2}$-oz) can deviled ham

2 tbsp sour cream
2 tbsp horseradish

Thinly slice tops from tomatoes. Remove pulp and drain shells upside down on paper towels. In small bowl combine remaining ingredients; fill tomatoes and refrigerate. Makes approximately 20.

Sausage-Cheese Balls

1½ c all-purpose
    baking/biscuit mix
16 oz or 4 c shredded sharp
    cheddar cheese

2 lb ground pork sausage
½ c finely onion, chopped
½ c celery, finely chopped
½ tsp garlic powder

Mix all ingredients and roll into 1-inch balls. Bake 15 minutes on ungreased cookie sheet at 375°, until golden brown. Makes about 6 dozen.

Cheese Puffs

¾ c margarine or butter
1 (3-oz) pkg cream cheese
8 oz sharp cheddar cheese
Tabasco sauce
Garlic salt
Worcestershire sauce

2 egg whites beaten
    stiffly
1 white sandwich
    loaf of bread
    (frozen)

Melt butter or margarine and cheeses together. Add seasoning. Fold in beaten egg whites.

    Cut crusts off frozen loaf. Cut bread in cubes and dip each cube in cheese mixture. Place on greased cookie sheet and set in fridge overnight. Bake at 350° for 15 minutes.

Honey-Soy Chicken Wings or Ribs

½ c honey
¼ c soy sauce
1 clove garlic, crushed

1 tbsp ketchup
Seasoning salt, to taste

Mix and marinate ribs or chicken for at least 2 hours. Bake at 350°
for ¾ hour on foil-lined baking sheet, turning once.

Chinese Chicken

1 can crushed pineapple
½ c water
½ c vinegar

½ c brown sugar
Cornstarch

Mix and thicken with cornstarch. Baste chicken wings or drumettes
for 2 hours. Bake at 350° for 45 minutes on foil-lined baking sheet,
turning once.

Cocktail Meatballs

1 lb ground beef
1 egg
½ c bread crumbs
½ c ketchup

1 tbsp parsley flakes
½ tsp onion powder
½ tsp seasoned salt
Pinch pepper

SAUCE:

1 (14-oz) bottle hot or
   regular ketchup

1 (12-oz) jar apple jelly
1 (12-oz) jar currant jelly
2 tbsp cornstarch

In a bowl combine meatball ingredients. Mix well and shape into 1-inch balls. Place on a rack in a shallow pan. Bake at 350° for 10–15 minutes. Combine ketchup and cornstarch. Stir in jellies. Place on top of meatballs.

Magic Meatball Sauce

1 (1-lb 10-oz) jar of Ragu, traditional recipe
1 (18-oz) bottle Kraft Spicy Honey BBQ sauce
1 can cream of chicken soup

Melt can of soup over low fire or in microwave. It is almost solid and will cause your sauce to be lumpy if you don't melt it first. Add all ingredients into Crock-Pot and add cooked, defrosted meatballs. Simmer until ready to eat.

Toasties

1¼ lb lean ground beef
½ c grated cheese
½ c green pepper, chopped
1 can mushrooms, drained
1 can cream of mushroom soup
¾ c bread crumbs
½ c onion, chopped

1 egg
Dash of
    Worcestershire
    sauce
Salt and pepper
Slices of bread
Butter

Mix well all except for last 2 ingredients. Using a cup or round cookie cutter, slice bread into rounds. Butter one side of rounds and put buttered side down in muffin tins. Add mixture and bake at 375° for approximately 25 minutes. Makes 42 toasties.

Bologna Bites

Place a piece of bologna on top of a microwave-safe cup. Microwave 30 seconds. Let cool.

When you flip it up, you have a little container. Stuff with grated cheese, beans, eggs, veggies, croutons, and a creamy dip, etc. Use your imagination!

No-Crust Quiche

2 c grated cheese (cheddar or
  Swiss)
1 onion, coarsely chopped
2 (10-oz) cans sliced
  mushrooms (drained)

2 tbsp butter
16 Ritz crackers
8 eggs
Salt and pepper to taste

Sauté onion and mushrooms in butter. Crush crackers. Add remaining ingredients, except mushrooms and onions which are added at the end. Fill muffin tins ½ full or use two 9-inch pie plates and bake at 325° for 35 minutes.

OPTIONS:
You can add 8–10 slices bacon, fried and crushed, or shrimp pieces.

Cheddar-Bacon Truffles

6 slices side bacon, chopped
8 oz old cheddar cheese, cubed
¼ c butter, cubed
2 tbsp each parsley and green
    onions, chopped

2 tbsp drained hot banana
    pepper rings, or to
    taste
¾ c toasted pecans, finely
    chopped

Cook bacon until crisp, drain well, reserving 1 tablespoon drippings, and set aside. Combine cheese, butter, parsley, green onions, and banana pepper rings and blend in food processor. Add bacon and drippings and process until bacon is finely chopped. Chill mixture 3 hours or until firm enough to roll into 2 dozen balls, 1 inch in diameter. If mixture softens during rolling, return to refrigerator. Roll balls in chopped pecans and store in refrigerator up to 2 days before serving. Serve with crackers.

Hot Mushroom Turnovers

1 (8-oz) pkg cream cheese,
  softened
All-purpose flour
Butter or margarine, softened
½ lb mushrooms, minced

1 large onion,
  minced
¼ c sour cream
1 tsp salt
¼ tsp thyme leaves
1 egg, beaten

About 2 hours before serving, in a large bowl beat cream cheese, add 1½ cups flour, and ½ cup butter, mix until smooth. Shape into ball, wrap, and refrigerate 1 hour.

In 10-inch skillet over medium heat, put 3 tablespoons butter, and cook mushrooms, and onion until tender, stirring occasionally. Stir in sour cream, salt, thyme, and 2 tablespoons flour; set aside.

On floured surface with floured rolling pin, roll half of dough ⅛-inch thick. With floured 2¾-inch round cookie cutter, cut out as many circles as possible. Repeat.

Preheat oven to 450°. On one half of each dough circle, place a teaspoon of mushroom mixture. Brush edges of circles with some egg; fold dough over filling. With fork, firmly press edges together to seal then prick tops. Place turnovers on ungreased cookie sheet and brush with remaining egg. Bake 12 to 14 minutes until golden. Makes about 3½ dozen.

Hot Crab Triangles

1 (8-oz) pkg cream cheese, softened
1/2 tsp dry mustard
1 tbsp milk
Dash cayenne
1 (6-oz) can white crabmeat, drained
2 tbsp minced chives or green onion
2 tbsp blanched almonds, finely chopped
12 slices firm-type white bread, crusts trimmed
Paprika

Beat cream cheese, mustard, and milk until fluffy. Add cayenne, crab, onion or chives and mix well. Add almonds and mix again. Spread generously on bread slices. Sprinkle lightly with paprika. Cut each slice in 4 triangles and put on baking sheet. Bake at 400° 10–12 minutes, or until well browned. Serve on cocktail picks. Makes 4 dozen.

Teriyaki Meatballs

2 eggs
2 lb ground round steak
½ c cornflake crumbs
½ c milk

2 tbsp grated onion
1 tsp salt
¼ tsp pepper

Mix and form into meatballs, about 1½ inches in diameter, and bake 45 minutes at 300°, turning and braising every 15 minutes.

SAUCE:

1 c soy sauce
2 tsp ginger juice or 1 tsp
   powdered ginger

½ c water
2 cloves garlic,
   minced
1 tsp sugar

Combine and place over meatballs, cooking until heated through.

Stuffed Bacon Rolls

¹/₄ c milk
1 egg, beaten
2 c soft bread crumbs,
   about 3 slices
10 or 11 slices bacon

1 c Granny Smith apple,
   finely chopped
1 tbsp onion, finely
   chopped
1 tbsp parsley, snipped
Salt and pepper to taste

In a mixing bowl, combine milk and egg. Add crumbs, apple, onion, parsley, salt, and pepper; mix well.

   Cut each slice of bacon in half crosswise. Shape crumb mixture into balls, using one rounded tablespoon for each. Wrap each ball in half bacon slice; secure with a wooden pick. Place on a wire rack set in a 15x10x1-inch baking pan. Bake at 375° for 30 minutes or until bacon is brown. Makes 20–22.

Shrimp-Bacon Bites

1 c cleaned cooked shrimp, or 1 can
¹/₂ clove garlic, slivered

¹/₂ c chili sauce
8 to 10 slices bacon

Mix shrimp and garlic; pour chili sauce over mixture. Cover and refrigerate, stirring occasionally for several hours.

   Cut bacon slices into halves. Fry bacon until partially cooked; drain. Wrap each shrimp in bacon piece and secure with wooden pick. Broil 2–3 inches from heat until bacon is crisp. Makes 16–20.

Mushroom Treats

Fresh bread
3 tbsp onions, finely chopped
1/4 c butter
1/2 lb mushrooms, finely chopped
2 tbsp flour
1 c heavy cream

1/2 tsp salt
1/8 tsp cayenne
1 tbsp parsley
1 tbsp chives
1/2 tsp lemon juice
Parmesan cheese

Using a cup, cut bread into circles the size of a muffin tin. Press bread lightly into bottoms of muffin tins and bake 10 minutes at 400°.

Sauté onions in butter. Add mushrooms and cook on low heat 10–15 minutes. Remove from heat and add flour and cream; bring to a boil and simmer 1–2 minutes. Add spices and lemon juice, and let cool.

Fill cups with mixture; put a dot of butter on top and sprinkle with Parmesan cheese. Bake at 350° for 10 minutes (broil for 1 minute if needed). Makes 4 dozen.

Pasta Rolls

FILLING:

1 (8-oz) pkg plain cream cheese, softened

4 oz sharp cheddar cheese, shredded

Dash cayenne pepper

$^1/_2$ c chopped unsalted cashews, lightly toasted

2 tbsp parsley, finely chopped

Combine cheeses and cayenne and beat until smooth. Stir in nuts and parsley.

ROLLS:

Remove crusts from slices of fresh bread. Roll with rolling pin to flatten and thin. Butter the bread slightly and spread filling to the edges. Roll up jelly-roll fashion or make small sandwich fingers or squares. To store, wrap well in plastic wrap and freeze no longer than 2 weeks.

Cheese Pitas

¹/₂ pt cottage cheese
4 oz ricotta cheese
1 oz feta cheese
1 egg
¹/₂ green onion, chopped

1 tbsp minced
    parsley
6 sheets filo dough
2 tbsp melted butter

Beat together cheeses, egg, onion, and parsley. Lay out the filo dough and cover with plastic wrap. Using one sheet at a time, brush lightly with butter. Cut each sheet into 6 strips about 3 inches wide. Place a teaspoon of filling at one end of each strip. Fold like a flag (folding/rolling in triangles to capture filling in middle, layering filo around it).

Place seam down on greased baking sheet. Brush tops with melted butter. Bake at 350° for 15 minutes or until golden brown. Makes approximately 3 dozen.

Swiss Cheese and Ham Tartlets

2 c finely shredded
  Swiss cheese
$^2/_3$ c cooked ham, finely
  chopped
$^1/_3$ c green onion, chopped

$^1/_3$ c sour cream
24 frozen unbaked
  3-inch tart shells
Salt and pepper to
  taste

Combine cheese, ham, onions, and sour cream and mix well. Add salt and pepper. Place tart shells on large baking sheet. Bake at 375° for 10 minutes only. Remove from oven and divide cheese mixture evenly among shells. Return to oven and bake 10 minutes more or until filling is hot and melted.

Coconut Shrimp

SHRIMP:

1 pouch shaker chicken
   coating mix
1 c coconut, toasted
$\frac{1}{2}$ tsp curry powder

$\frac{1}{4}$ tsp cayenne pepper
1 lb shrimp, fresh or
   frozen, thawed
1 egg, beaten

Combine dry ingredients. Dip shrimp in beaten egg, then into coating mixture. Bake 10–12 minutes at 400°.

CURRY DIP:

$\frac{1}{2}$ c ranch salad dressing
$\frac{1}{4}$ c orange marmalade

1 tsp curry
2–3 drops hot pepper
   sauce, if desired

Stir together. Refrigerate until ready to use.

Sauerkraut Balls

½ lb pork sausage meat
⅓ c onion, finely chopped
1 tbsp flour
14 oz canned sauerkraut,
    well drained, finely chopped
4 oz cream cheese, softened
1 tsp prepared mustard
1 tsp parsley flakes

⅛ tsp salt
¼ tsp garlic powder
¼ tsp pepper
⅓ c flour
2 large eggs
2 tbsp water
1 c fine bread crumbs
Fat, for deep frying

Fry sausage meat and onion in frying pan until no pink remains and onion is soft. Sprinkle flour over top; mix. Add sauerkraut, cream cheese, mustard, parsley, salt, garlic powder, and pepper. Stir until blended. Chill until it will hold its shape. Roll into 1-inch balls.

Put flour in one bowl, beaten eggs in another bowl, and bread crumbs in another. Roll balls first in flour, then in eggs, then in bread crumbs, until coated.

Carefully drop balls one at a time in hot oil or fat. Deep-fry until browned, about 3 minutes. Remove with slotted spoon to tray lined with paper towels to drain. Serve warm. Makes approximately 30.

Dried Garlic Spareribs

1 lb spareribs, chopped in
   1-inch squares
Pinch gourmet powder
2 tbsp Chinese cooking wine
2 tbsp light soy sauce
1 tbsp sugar

⅛ tsp salt or garlic
   salt
3–4 cloves minced
   garlic
Dash pepper
A few drops sesame
   oil

Marinate spareribs with 1 tablespoon cooking wine, 1 table-spoon soy sauce, and gourmet powder for 30 minutes. Deep-fry in hot oil for 5 minutes. Remove to a plate.

Using a hot wok, add 1 tablespoon peanut oil until almost smoky. Put in minced garlic to brown for a few seconds, then add spareribs, sugar, pepper, garlic salt, remainder of cooking wine and soy sauce, and sesame oil. Stir-fry for 3 minutes over medium heat. Serve.

Beverages

*"I tell you the truth,
anyone who gives you a
cup of water in my name
because you belong to Christ
will certainly not lose his reward."*

MARK 9:41

Fresh Berry Punch

1 (12-oz) bag fresh cranberries
3 c water
1 envelope raspberry
   beverage mix

1 can thawed pineapple juice
   concentrate
1 large banana, mashed
1 large bottle ginger ale

Puree 2 cups cranberries. Combine pureed cranberries, remaining whole cranberries, and water in large saucepan. Cook over high heat until cranberries begin to pop; remove from heat. Stir in remaining ingredients except ginger ale. Freeze about 12 hours, stir, and refreeze.

To serve:
Puree slush in food processor, spoon into pitcher, and mix in ginger ale.

Fruit Punch

10 c sugar
10 c water
2 doz lemons

1 doz oranges
1 can pineapple, grapefruit,
   or grape juice

Make syrup of water, sugar, and rind of 3 lemons and 3 oranges. Boil 10 minutes. Cool, add fruit juices, and strain. Dilute as required.

Cranberry Juice

4 c cranberries
4 c water

$^2/_3$ c sugar or
    1 c corn syrup

Cook cranberries until skins pop open. Strain through cheesecloth. Heat, add sugar, and boil for 2 minutes. Chill before serving. Lemon, orange, grapefruit, or pineapple juice may be combined with this.

Slush

1 (48-oz) can pineapple juice
1 (12-oz) can frozen orange juice
    concentrate (thawed and
    undiluted)

2 (6-oz) cans frozen
    lemonade concentrate
    (thawed and undiluted)

Mix all ingredients together and store in freezer in ice-cream pail. When serving, place slush in bottom of a tall glass and fill with 7-Up or ginger ale. Garnish with maraschino cherry.

Hot Cappuccino

1 c instant hot chocolate
mix powder
½ c instant coffee granules
(good quality)
½ c powdered nondairy
coffee whitener
½ c skim milk powder

1¼ tsp ground
cinnamon
¼ tsp ground
nutmeg
Boiling water
Grated chocolate
(optional)

Mix dry ingredients well. Use ¼ cup mixture for each 2 cups boiling water. Put desired amount in blender until foamy and pour into mugs. May be sprinkled with grated chocolate if desired.

Wassail Punch

2 qt apple cider
2 c orange juice
2 c pineapple juice
½ c lemon juice

½ c sugar
12 cloves, whole
4 cinnamon sticks,
3–4" long

Bring all ingredients to a boil. Reduce heat. Simmer 10–15 minutes. Remove cloves and cinnamon sticks. Serve warm. Makes 3½ quarts.

Holiday Punch

2 c cranberry cocktail
4 c lemonade
1 c orange juice

Maraschino cherries
Lemon slices
3 (6-oz) bottles of
    ginger ale

Mix all ingredients (except ginger ale) together in a large bowl. Chill. Add ginger ale just before serving. Yields 18 punch cups.

Cranberry-Orange Punch

1 (6-oz) can frozen orange
    juice concentrate,
    reconstituted (3 c)

1³/₄ c cranberry juice
    cocktail, chilled
1 (12-oz) bottle
    ginger ale, chilled

Combine juices in large pitcher or small punch bowl with ice. Stir in ginger ale just before serving. Makes 6½ cups.

Three-Fruit Punch

1 (6-oz) can frozen lemonade
   concentrate
1 (10-oz) pkg frozen strawberries,
   thawed

1 (8-oz) can crushed
   pineapple
3 qt cold ginger ale
Crushed ice

Blend lemonade, pineapple, and strawberries until smooth (can be made in advance and refrigerated). Combine with ginger ale and ice. Makes 1 gallon.

Apple Juice Nog

3 c pure apple juice
3 eggs
2 c vanilla ice cream

$1/4$ tsp cinnamon
Nutmeg

Combine all ingredients except nutmeg in blender container. Cover and blend until smooth, and chill. Pour into glasses and sprinkle with nutmeg.

Tahitian Punch

1 can pineapple juice, chilled
1 can orange-grapefruit juice, chilled
1 pt lemon or lime sherbet

2 qt carbonated lemon-lime beverage, chilled

In large punch bowl, stir together juices and carbonated beverage. Spoon sherbet into bowl. Serve immediately. Garnish with citrus slices and a sprig of mint if desired.

Golden Glow Punch

3 c unsweetened pineapple juice
3 large bottles 7-Up or ginger ale

1 qt orange juice
1 c lemon juice

Mix and serve with sliced oranges and maraschino cherries if desired.

Spiced Tea

4 tea bags orange pekoe tea
Juice of 3 oranges and 3 lemons
4 tsp cinnamon

1½ tsp cloves
2 c sugar
1 gal water (16 c)

Simmer 20 minutes and remove tea bags.

Candies/
Confectioneries/
Sweets

*Eat honey, my son, for it is good;
honey from the comb is sweet to your taste.*

PROVERBS 24:13

Almond Florentine

Graham wafers
1 c butter
1 c brown sugar

1 c flaked almonds
Honey (optional)

Layer wafers on cookie sheet and set aside. Melt butter and brown sugar, add honey if desired, and cook over medium heat for 5 minutes—*Do not boil*. Spoon mixture over wafers. Sprinkle almonds on top. Bake at 350° for 10 minutes.

Christmas Fruit Balls

1 bag mini marshmallows
2 c graham wafer crumbs
1/2 c red maraschino cherries, halved

1/2 c green maraschino cherries, halved
1 (15-oz) can sweetened condensed milk
1/2 c walnuts, chopped

Mix together everything but the coconut. Chill overnight. Shape chilled mixture into balls which are about 1 inch in diameter, then roll in coconut. Store in a covered container in refrigerator. Makes 4 dozen balls.

Peppermint Jells

1 box Certo Crystals powdered
    fruit pectin
$^3/_4$ c water
$^1/_2$ tsp baking soda

1 c icing sugar
1 c light corn syrup
10 drops green food coloring
$^1/_2$ tsp peppermint extract
$^1/_2$ c icing sugar

Mix pectin, water, and soda (mixture will foam slightly) in a 2-quart saucepan. In separate pan, mix sugar and corn syrup. Heat both mixtures at the same time, stirring constantly until foam has disappeared from pectin mixture and sugar mixture is boiling rapidly (3–5 minutes). Pour pectin mixture in a slow steady stream into sugar mixture, stirring constantly. Be careful and use a long-handled spoon; this superboils at the time the 2 liquids are mixed. Boil and stir 1 minute longer. Remove from heat and stir in coloring and flavoring. Pour into $9^1/_2$x$5^1/_4$-inch loaf pan or 8x8-inch square pan. Let stand at room temperature until cool and firm. Cut into $^3/_4$-inch squares and roll in icing sugar. Let stand at room temperature overnight.

VARIATIONS:

CINNAMON: 15 drops red food coloring, 4 drops cinnamon or
    cassia oil
ORANGE: 10 drops orange food coloring, $1^1/_2$ to 2 tsp orange
    extract

Just Like an O'Henry Bar

12 oz chocolate chips
12 oz butterscotch chips

2 c dry Chinese chow-mein
noodles
2 c unsalted peanuts

Melt the chocolate in double boiler and add the rest of the ingredients. Drop on waxed paper and refrigerate.

Caramel Creams

3 c white sugar
1 c corn syrup

1 c sweet cream

Boil gently 10–15 minutes or until a small quantity dropped in cold water forms a firm ball. Beat until thick and cool enough to handle.

There are 3 options to shape/finish.

Roll in small balls and dip in melted semisweet chocolate; add 3–4 drops oil of peppermint, pour into pan, cut in squares; or shape into cylinders about 1 inch in diameter, roll in chopped pecans, and slice.

Christmas Fudge

3 c sugar
½ c boiling water (for
   colored fudge, use the
   liquid from the cherries)
½ c corn syrup

2 egg whites
1 tsp vanilla
1 small bottle green
   or red cherries,
   cut fine

Combine syrup, sugar, and water. Boil until syrup forms hard ball when dropped on ice. Pour gradually over egg whites which have been beaten stiff. Continue beating until mixture holds shape. Add cherries during beating. Pour into buttered pan and cut when cool.

Chocolate Snowballs

Note: This sounds strange, but they are delicious!
No one will ever know what they're made of!

1 medium hot mashed potato
2–3 c icing sugar
Vanilla

Chocolate
Coconut or chopped
   nuts

Mix 1 cup icing sugar into the mashed potato; add vanilla. Mix in additional icing sugar until it makes a soft dough. Roll into balls and let set. Dip in melted chocolate and roll in coconut or chopped nuts.

Maple Crisps

1 c shortening
2 c brown sugar, packed
1 tsp maple extract
2 eggs
3½ c flour

¼ tsp salt
1 tsp soda
1 c almonds,
    blanched and
    chopped

Cream shortening, sugar, and maple extract. Add eggs and mix well. Add flour, salt, and soda. Mix in almonds; combine thoroughly. Roll or cut cookies. Bake at 400° for 6–8 minutes. Store in loosely covered tin to keep crisp.

Porcupines

1 c dates, chopped
1 c nuts, chopped
1½ c coconut, plus extra for
    rolling

1 c brown sugar
1 tbsp butter
2 eggs
1 tsp vanilla

Mix dates, nuts, and coconut. Blend in butter, eggs, and vanilla. Roll into balls, then roll in additional coconut. Bake at 325° for 18–20 minutes. Makes 5 dozen.

Christmas Soft Candies

1 can Eagle Brand milk
2 lb icing sugar
Flavoring—pick one of peppermint,
    almond, maple, or vanilla—or
    divide dough for a variety

Nuts, dates, or cherries
6 squares semisweet or
    unsweetened chocolate
1½ tbsp paraffin wax

Mix canned milk and icing sugar to make a dough. Either mix the entire batch with one type of flavoring, or divide for a variety. Add nuts, dates, or cherries to the base and roll into tiny balls. Set to cool. Melt wax and chocolate in double boiler. Using a toothpick, dip in candies to coat. Put on cookie sheet to harden.

Snookie Cookies

½ c broken walnuts
½ c dates
½ lb colored marshmallows,
    cut in pieces

½ c unsweetened
    condensed milk
¼ c boiling water
2½ c graham wafer crumbs

Mix first 4 ingredients and pour boiling water over them. Stir in wafer crumbs. Make into a roll about 2 inches thick. Let stand overnight. Cut into slices.

Quick Chocolate Drops

3 c quick oats
1 c shredded coconut
6 tbsp cocoa
½ c butter

½ c milk
2 c white sugar
½ tsp vanilla

Mix oats, coconut, and cocoa. Heat butter, milk, and sugar together in a saucepan until almost to the boiling point, but do not boil. Pour over dry mixture and stir well. Drop by spoonfuls on buttered waxed paper. Chill until firm.

Brigadeiras

(pronounced Brig-uh-DAY-ruz)

1 can sweetened condensed milk
4 tbsp butter or margarine
2 tbsp cocoa or Nesquik
Sugar, chocolate, or colored sprinkles

Melt butter in a pan. Add other ingredients and cook over medium heat. Cook and stir constantly until really thick—about 5 or 10 minutes—until you see the bottom of the pan easily. Let cool. Roll into balls quickly. Then roll in sugar, chocolate, or colored sprinkles. Makes 2–3 dozen.

Peanut Butter Fudge

$^3/_4$ c butter or $1^1/_2$ sticks
   margarine
3 c sugar
1 (5-oz) can or $^2/_3$ c
   evaporated milk
$^1/_2$ pkg (about 5 oz)
   peanut butter chips

$^1/_2$ pkg. (about 6 oz)
   semisweet chocolate
   chips
1 (7-oz) jar
   marshmallow creme
1 tsp vanilla

Lightly grease 13x9-inch or 9-inch square pan. Mix margarine, sugar, and milk in a heavy saucepan. Bring to full, rolling boil over medium heat, stirring constantly. Continue boiling for 5 minutes on medium heat, stirring constantly to prevent scorching. Remove from heat. Gradually stir in chips until melted. Add marshmallow creme and vanilla. Mix well. Pour into prepared pan. Cool at room temperature. Cut into squares.

No-Bake Christmas Graham Fudge

1 (12-oz) pkg semisweet
  chocolate chips
¼ c butter or margarine
2½ c graham cracker crumbs

1½ c almonds or pecans,
  chopped
1 (14-oz) can sweetened
  condensed milk
1 tsp vanilla

Melt chocolate chips and butter together until smooth. In large bowl, combine graham crumbs and nuts. Stir in condensed milk and vanilla until crumbs are moistened, then stir in chocolate mixture until mixed. Pat evenly in greased 12x8-inch pan. Let stand at room temperature 2 hours before cutting.

Toffee

1 c butter
1¼ c brown sugar
3 tbsp corn syrup

3 tbsp water
1½ c whole almonds
Chocolate chips, to taste

Bake almonds at 375° for 10 minutes on baking sheet. Turn off and leave in oven.

Cook first 4 ingredients over medium heat stirring constantly until mixture reaches 300° (hard crack) on candy thermometer.

Spread candy on cookie sheet with nuts (work fast). Cool. Melt chocolate chips, drizzle or coat, to taste. Crack.

Cookies

Nehemiah said,
"Go and enjoy choice food and sweet drinks,
and send some to
those who have nothing prepared.
This day is sacred to our Lord.
Do not grieve,
for the joy of the LORD is your strength."

NEHEMIAH 8:10

Merry Fruit Cookies

1½ c mixed fruit, glazed
2 eggs
½ c dates, chopped
¼ c flour
¾ c dark raisins
½ lb butter

1 c sugar
½ tsp almond flavoring
½ tsp baking powder
½ tsp baking soda
½ tsp ground cinnamon
2¼ c flour

Place fruit, raisins, dates, and ¼ cup flour in bowl; stir to coat fruit with flour. Cream margarine and sugar in another bowl. Add eggs one at a time, beating well after each addition. Add flavoring. Stir dry ingredients; add fruit mixture and stir. Add to batter. Stir until it is too difficult to mix. Work with hands until flour is mixed in. Shape into 2 or 3 logs about 1½ inches in diameter. Roll each log in waxed paper and chill for 1 hour or longer. Cut into ¼-inch slices. Arrange ½ inch apart; bake at 375° for 10 minutes until golden. Makes 4–5 dozen.

Snickerdoodles

2 c sugar
2 eggs, well beaten
½ c butter, softened
1 tsp vanilla
4 c flour

4 tsp baking powder
1 tsp salt
1 c milk
1 c raisins
Cinnamon and sugar for
    garnish

Gradually add sugar to eggs. Stir in butter and mix well. Add vanilla. Mix dry ingredients and add alternately to the egg mixture with the milk, beating well between additions. Stir in raisins. Drop by teaspoons onto a greased cookie sheet, about an inch apart. Sprinkle with cinnamon and sugar. Bake 10–12 minutes at 375°.

Cherry Christmas Cookies

1 c soft butter
¾ c brown sugar
½ tsp vanilla
⅛ tsp salt

2½ c flour
1 c sliced almonds
½ c red cherries, whole
½ c green cherries, whole

Cream butter, add sugar and then vanilla, salt, and flour. Finally, add nuts and cherries and form into rolls. Leave in fridge overnight. Slice thinly with a sharp knife and bake on greased baking sheet at 375° for 10 minutes.

Cracker Jack Cookies

1 c butter
1 c white sugar
1 c brown sugar
2 tsp vanilla
1½ c flour
1 tsp baking powder

1 tsp baking soda
2 c oatmeal
1 c coconut
2 c Rice Krispies
2 eggs

Cream butter; add sugar, eggs, and vanilla and cream well. Combine dry ingredients and mix all together. Stir in oatmeal, coconut, and Rice Krispies by hand. Drop by teaspoonfuls onto greased cookie sheet. Bake at 350° for 10–12 minutes until nicely browned.

Shortbread

1 lb butter
1 c icing sugar
1 c cornstarch

3 c flour
Pinch of salt
A few drops of lemon juice

Cream butter, gradually add remaining ingredients, but do not over-beat. Press cookies onto ungreased baking sheet, using a cookie press. Bake at 275° for approximately 25 minutes, or until just slightly brown at bottom.

Hazelnut Meringue Cookies

2 egg whites
½ c granulated sugar
½ tsp vanilla

½ tsp vinegar
⅛ tsp salt
1 c hazelnuts

Line baking sheets with either brown paper or parchment paper. Beat egg whites until soft peaks form. Gradually add sugar and salt; continue beating for 3–4 minutes until meringue is very stiff, and sugar has dissolved. Beat in vanilla and vinegar. Fold in hazelnuts.

Drop by spoonfuls in small mounds (about 1½ inches) on prepared baking sheets. Bake in 300° oven for 30 minutes or until light brown. Turn off heat. Leave in oven until oven is cool or overnight to thoroughly dry. Lift off paper. Makes 24 cookies.

Cherry Flips

1 c butter
½ c icing sugar
2 egg yolks
2 c sifted cake flour
¼ tsp salt

2 tsp almond flavoring
30 maraschino cherries
    (save juice)
Crushed nuts or
    shredded coconut

Cream butter and sugar; add egg yolks and beat well. Blend in flour and salt; add flavoring. Pinch off pieces and roll out flat in your hand. Insert a cherry and fold the dough around it to form a ball. Bake on a greased baking sheet at 325° for 25 minutes or until light brown.

When cold, dip in thin icing made from 1½ cups icing sugar and ½ cup cherry juice. Roll in nuts or coconut.

Candy Cane Sugar Cookies

1 c sugar
1 c butter, softened
½ c milk
1 egg
1 tsp vanilla
1 tsp almond extract

3½ c flour
1 tsp baking powder
¼ tsp salt
½ tsp red food coloring
Crushed candy canes, to taste

Mix sugar, butter, milk, egg, vanilla, and almond extract. Stir in flour, baking powder, and salt. Divide dough into half. Tint one half with red food coloring. Cover and refrigerate at least 4 hours.

One at a time, roll both colors into ropes. Press 1 white and 1 pink rope together, then twist together. Cut into 8-inch lengths, then curl one end over to make the shape of a candy cane, being careful not to let the dough "break" as you make the shape. Sprinkle with crushed candy canes; bake at 375° for 9–12 minutes. Do not overbake.

VARIATION: Tint one half green, twist, and join ropes into circles to make wreaths. Decorate with cut maraschino cherries.

Christmas Macaroons

3 egg whites
1 c fine granulated sugar
1 tbsp cornstarch
Pinch of salt
1 c coconut

$\frac{1}{2}$ c candied cherries,
   cut in pieces
$\frac{1}{4}$ c almonds, blanched
   and cut in pieces

Beat the egg whites until stiff but not dry. Mix sugar, salt, and corn-starch and add gradually, beating constantly. Cook in a double boiler until a crust forms. Remove from heat. Fold in fruit and nuts. Roll into small balls. Bake on well-greased baking sheet at 300° until firm and slightly brown, about 20–30 minutes. Makes about 3 dozen.

Dips

" "*Bring the fattened calf and kill it.*
Let's have a feast and celebrate.' "

LUKE 15:23

Imitation Crab Dip

1 c sour cream
1 c mayonnaise
1 pkg Knorr vegetable soup

1 (6-oz) can water
   chestnuts, drained
   and chopped
6–8 oz imitation crab

Mix and chill overnight. Serve with crackers.

Crab Dip

8 oz cream cheese
2 tsp mayonnaise
2 tsp Worcestershire sauce
1 small onion, grated

2 tsp lemon juice
1 bottle Heinz chili sauce
1 can crabmeat
Parsley flakes

Mix first 5 ingredients until smooth. Spread in pan. Pour chili sauce over. Drain crab. Spread over. Sprinkle with parsley. Set in refrigerator at least 3 hours; serve with crackers.

Taco Dip

4 oz cream cheese

Spread over 13-inch plate.

LAYER THE FOLLOWING ON TOP:

1 lb cooked ground beef
1 pkg sour cream
1 envelope taco seasoning
1 can tomato paste
1 tomato, chopped

2–3 green onions
Shredded cheddar cheese,
  to taste
Chopped lettuce, to taste

Serve with taco chips.

Party Ham Spread

BLEND AND CHILL:

2 cans flaked ham
1/2 c mayonnaise
2 hard-boiled eggs

2 tbsp minced onion
1/4 c relish

Serve with party crackers.

Mexican Dip

1 lb cooked ground beef
½ c green pepper, chopped
2 cloves garlic, chopped
1 onion, chopped

1 pkg taco seasoning
1 can refried beans
1½ c mild salsa
2–3 c shredded cheese
Taco chips or taco
   shells

Preheat oven to 350°. Fry beef in a skillet and drain. Add onion, green pepper, and garlic. Simmer 10 minutes. Spread refried beans over 9x13-inch casserole dish. Spread beef mixture on top, then sour cream. Top with cheese. Bake for 35 minutes or until browned. Serve with taco chips or roll in soft taco shells.

Shrimp Spread

1 can tiny shrimp
1 (4-oz) pkg cream cheese,
   softened

1 clove garlic, minced
Lemon juice
Cayenne pepper

Coarsely chop the shrimp. Add the cream cheese, a few drops of lemon juice, and garlic to taste. Mix, cover, and chill. Sprinkle with cayenne pepper and serve with crackers.

Easy Taco Dip

1 (8-oz) pkg cream cheese,
  softened

1 c sour cream
1 pkg dry taco mix,
  or to taste

Combine ingredients and spread in shallow, round dish.

Combine 1 cup each: chopped iceberg lettuce and chopped tomatoes, drained. Top with chopped green onions and shredded cheddar cheese. Serve with taco chips.

Shrimp Mold

1 envelope gelatin
1/2 c tomato soup, undiluted
1 can shrimp pieces
1/2 c celery, cut fine
1/4 c green onions, cut fine

3/4 c mayonnaise or salad
  dressing
1 (8-oz) pkg cream
  cheese, softened

Dissolve gelatin in 2 tablespoons cold water. Heat tomato soup and mix together. Add balance of ingredients, mix, and pour into mold or plastic bowl. Let set overnight. Serve with crackers.

Fresh Vegetables with Savory Dip

Fresh vegetables
1 (4-oz) pkg of cream
   cheese, softened
2 tbsp milk
½ tsp Dijon mustard
½ tsp dried Italian seasoning

1 tbsp parsley, chopped
   or 1 tsp dried parsley
   flakes
1 small clove garlic,
   minced

Combine all ingredients except vegetables and spoon into small serving bowl. Prepare a variety of vegetables. Place dip in center of platter and surround with vegetables.

Easy Cracker Dip

LAYER IN ROUND DISH:

1 (8-oz) pkg cream cheese,
   softened
1 small jar cocktail sauce

1 can small shrimp or
   crabmeat

Serve with crackers.

Spinach Dip

1 pkg frozen spinach,
  (uncooked)
2 c sour cream
1 c mayonnaise

1 pkg Knorr vegetable soup
1 can water chestnuts
$1/3$ c green onions, chopped
1 large pumpernickel bread

Dry and finely chop spinach. Drain water chestnuts and finely chop. Blend all ingredients together. Cut off top of pumpernickel bread and scoop out inside. Fill with dip. Use top and inside of bread as well as crackers and vegetables for dipping.

Christmas Party Shrimp Spread

1 can broken shrimp
1 (8-oz) pkg cream cheese,
  softened
2 tbsp mayonnaise
1 tbsp ketchup

$1/2$ tsp prepared mustard
Dash of garlic powder
  (optional)
Chopped celery or green
  onions (optional)

Cream the cream cheese, mayonnaise, ketchup, mustard, and garlic powder. Add mashed and drained shrimp; mix well. Add garlic, celery, and/or green onions if desired. Refrigerate.

64

Cheese Ball

1 (8-oz) pkg cream cheese, softened
2½ c sharp cheddar cheese, grated
½ c dill pickles, chopped
½ c walnuts, finely chopped

¼ c green onions, finely chopped
2 tbsp Miracle Whip or mayonnaise
1 tsp Worcestershire sauce
Pinch of parsley, basil, and dill

Combine all the above except walnuts and spices, beating until smooth. Cover and chill until firm. Shape into a ball and roll into a mixture of walnuts, parsley, basil, and dill.

Low-Calorie Veggie Dip

1 c plain yogurt
¼ tsp salt
¼ tsp dill weed
⅛ tsp garlic salt

3 green onions, finely chopped
Dash of pepper
1 tsp honey

Combine all ingredients. Chill and serve with crackers.

Blue Cheese & Sun-Dried Tomato Spread

1 (8-oz) pkg cream cheese, room temperature
1/4 c sun-dried tomatoes in oil, drained, finely chopped
1/4 c crumbled blue cheese
1/4 c fresh parsley, chopped
1/4 c green pepper, finely chopped
1 tsp oregano
1 clove garlic, minced
Dash of freshly ground pepper

Combine all ingredients. Chill and serve with crackers or cocktail rye bread.

Cool Yogurt Dip

1 c plain low-fat yogurt
1/2 c grated cucumber, with peel
1/4–1/2 tsp salt
2 tbsp chopped fresh mint leaves, packed
1/4 tsp granulated sugar

Combine all ingredients and let stand at room temperature for 1 hour to meld flavors. Serve.

Tangy Cheese Spread

2 c finely shredded old
   cheddar cheese
Dash of garlic salt
1 tsp Dijon mustard

1 (4-oz) pkg cream
   cheese, softened
Dash of Tabasco sauce
Dash of Worcestershire
   sauce
$1/4$ c dry sherry

Using food processor or mixer, combine cheddar cheese, garlic salt, and Dijon mustard. Add cream cheese and blend until smooth. Add Tabasco, Worcestershire, and sherry. Beat until creamy. Spoon into serving dish, cover and chill for several days to blend flavors. Serve at room temperature with crackers.

Seafood Cracker Spread

1 (8-oz) pkg cream cheese
2 tbsp Thousand Island salad
   dressing
1 tin crabmeat

$1/4$–$1/2$ bottle chili sauce
   or seafood cocktail
   sauce
1 can shrimp

Mix cream cheese and salad dressing and spread on inner circle of dinner plate. Pour sauce over top. Crumble crab and shrimp meat and sprinkle on top. Serve with crackers.

Hot Crab Delight

1 (8-oz) pkg cream cheese at
   room temperature
1 (6½-oz) tin crabmeat
2 tbsp green onion, chopped
½ tsp horseradish

½ c slivered almonds
1 tbsp milk
½ tsp salt
1 tbsp lemon juice
Dash of pepper

Combine all ingredients except almonds; mix well. Garnish with almonds. Warm in oven at 350° for 20 minutes. Serve as a dip with crackers.

Surprise Spread

1 (8-oz) pkg cream cheese,
   softened

¼ c mayonnaise
½ c sour cream

Mix together and spread over a pizza pan-style plate.

ADD:

Woodman's Tangy Seafood
   Sauce
2 cans shrimp
2 c grated mozzarella cheese

1 c green peppers,
   chopped
3 green onions, chopped
1 tomato, diced

Sprinkle over cream mixture. Dip with crackers.

Homestyle Boursin

2 (8-oz) pkg softened cream
   cheese
¼ c mayonnaise
2 tsp Dijon mustard

1 clove garlic, minced
2 tbsp chives, finely chopped
2 tbsp fresh dill, finely
   chopped

Beat cheese, mayonnaise, mustard, chives, dill, and garlic with a mixer in a large bowl until thoroughly blended. Spoon into a small serving bowl or line a 2-cup mold with aluminum foil and spoon in mixture. Cover and refrigerate overnight. Turn out onto a small serving plate and peel off foil. Serve with crackers and vegetable dippers—celery sticks, cucumber slices, cherry tomatoes, zucchini, broccoli, and cauliflower florets.

Spicy Vegetable Dip

1 c sour cream
1 c mayonnaise
½ c chili sauce
1 tsp horseradish

1 tsp HP sauce or your
   favorite spicy steak
   sauce
1 tsp minced onion

Mix and serve.

Layered Bean Dip

2 (14-oz) cans refried beans
1 (4-oz) can green chiles,
    chopped
1 envelope taco seasoning mix
2 ripe avocados, peeled and
    pitted
2 jars taco sauce, mild,
    medium, or hot

2 tbsp lemon juice
$1\frac{1}{2}$ c sour cream
3 c shredded lettuce
$1\frac{1}{2}$ c shredded
    cheddar cheese
Black olives, sliced
    (optional)

Mix together refried beans, chiles, and taco seasoning. Spread on a
12-inch serving platter. Blend avocados, lemon juice, and $\frac{1}{2}$ cup taco
sauce until smooth and spread on top of bean mixture. Spread sour
cream on top of avocado mixture. Top with lettuce, cheese, remaining taco sauce, and olives if desired. Serve with taco chips.

Squares

*They are more precious than gold,
than much pure gold;
they are sweeter than honey,
than honey from the comb.*

PSALM 19:10

Butter Tart Squares

BASE:

1 c flour   ½ c butter
¼ c white sugar

Combine flour and sugar. Cut in butter until crumbly. Press into 9-inch pan. Bake at 350° for 15 minutes.

TOPPING:

2 tbsp butter, melted   ½ tsp vanilla
2 eggs   Pinch salt
1 c brown sugar   1 c raisins
2 tbsp flour   ½ c walnuts
½ tbsp baking powder

Mix together butter and eggs; blend in sugar, flour, baking powder, vanilla, and salt. Stir in raisins and walnuts. Pour over base. Bake at 350° for 20–30 minutes or until top springs back when touched lightly. Cool before cutting into squares.

Dream Slice

BASE:

½ c butter
1 c flour

Pinch of salt
2 tbsp brown sugar

Spread on 8x8-inch pan. Bake at 350° for 15 minutes.

TOPPING:

2 beaten eggs
1½ c brown sugar
4 tbsp flour
½ tsp baking powder

1 c walnuts, chopped
½ c coconut
½ c glazed cherries

Mix and pour on base; bake 20 minutes longer at 300°.

Peanut Butter-Marshmallow Slice

½ c butter
1 c peanut butter

2 (6-oz) pkg butterscotch
    chips
4 c miniature marshmallows

Melt first 3 ingredients in double boiler, then add marshmallows. Pour into greased 8x8-inch pan. Keep in refrigerator.

Maple Pecan Squares

BASE:

1 c flour

¼ c brown sugar
½ c butter

TOPPING:

⅔ c brown sugar
1 c maple syrup
2 eggs beaten
½ c soft butter

¼ tsp salt
⅔ c pecan halves
½ tsp vanilla
2 tbsp flour

Preheat oven to 350°. Rub flour, sugar, and butter together. Press mixture firmly into 7x11-inch pan. Bake at 350° for 5 minutes. Note: It should not be completely cooked. Combine sugar and syrup in a saucepan. Simmer 5 minutes. Cool lightly. Pour over beaten eggs, stirring. Stir in remaining ingredients. Spread over partially baked dough. Bake at 450° for 10 minutes then reduce heat to 350° for 20 minutes. Cool and cut into squares.

Cherry Slice

Graham wafers
1 pt whipped cream

1 pkg mini marshmallows
1 can cherry pie filling

Whip the cream, add mini marshmallows. Pour half of this mixture on wafers. Spread with pie filling. Pour remainder of cream mixture on top of cherries. Crumble 6 wafers and sprinkle on top. Refrigerate until serving.

Rocky Road Squares

BASE:

4 squares unsweetened
   chocolate
$^3/_4$ c butter
$1^1/_2$ c sugar

3 eggs
1 tbsp milk
1 c flour
1 c nuts, chopped

Heat chocolate and butter over low heat until butter melts. Stir until smooth, then stir in sugar. Mix in eggs and milk until well blended. Stir in flour and nuts. Spread in greased 9-inch square pan. Bake at 350° for 40 minutes. Add Rocky Road Topping and bake 10 minutes longer.

ROCKY ROAD TOPPING:

2 c miniature marshmallows
1 c semisweet chocolate chips

1 c nuts, chopped

Jam Bars

½ c butter
1 tbsp sugar
1 egg, beaten

1 c flour
1 tsp baking powder
Pinch salt

Mix and put in pan spread with jam.

TOPPING:

1 rounded tbsp butter
¾ c sugar
1 egg

1½ c coconut or crushed
   cornflakes
1 tsp vanilla

Beat sugar and butter together, add beaten egg, then stir in dry ingredients. Spread over top of base mixture. Bake 20–30 minutes or until top is nicely browned and thick.

Krispy Krunch Bars

2 c peanut butter
2½ c icing sugar
2½ c crisp rice cereal

¼ c butter or margarine
½ c walnuts, chopped
   (optional)

ICING:

⅔ c semisweet chocolate chips

1 tsp butter

Mix all ingredients except icing together in bowl. Press into 9x9-inch pan lined with waxed paper. Melt together chocolate chips and butter and spread on top. Makes 36 bars.

Butterscotch Oat Squares

2 c quick or instant oats
1 c brown sugar, packed
½ c melted butter

½ tsp vanilla
Melted chocolate (optional)

Combine oats and brown sugar. Mix well. Add melted butter and vanilla. Mix thoroughly. Divide mixture evenly into 2 ungreased 8-inch square pans. Spread and pat evenly. Bake at 375° for about 10 minutes or until golden. Squares will be soft but harden on cooling. Can be drizzled with melted chocolate, if desired. Allow to cool 5 minutes, then mark in squares with sharp knife. Loosen edges and allow to cool before removing from pans.

Brownies

1 c butter or margarine
4 tbsp cocoa
1½ c sugar
1 c flour

2 tsp baking powder
1 tsp vanilla
4 eggs
1 c walnuts, chopped

Melt butter or margarine in saucepan. Add cocoa, sugar, flour, baking powder, and walnuts. Add eggs one at a time, beating in well after each addition. Pour into greased 9x13-inch baking pan. Bake at 350° for 25–30 minutes. Ice with your favorite icing or sprinkle top with sifted icing sugar.

Almond Bars

1 c flour   ½ c butter
2 tbsp icing sugar

Press into a 9x9-inch pan. Bake at 350° for 15 minutes.

In double boiler, boil for 3 minutes:
4 tbsp butter   1 tsp vanilla
½ c brown sugar   ¼ c cream

Remove and add 1 cup sliced almonds, then spoon over base. Bake 15 minutes more.

Puffed Wheat Squares/Balls

½ c butter   1 tsp vanilla
½ c corn syrup   8 c puffed wheat for
1 c brown sugar   balls, 9 c for
2 tbsp cocoa   squares

In large pot, melt butter on medium heat and then add corn syrup, brown sugar, and cocoa and mix well. Increase heat slightly and once mixture starts to boil, let boil for only 30 seconds. Turn heat off and add the vanilla, then puffed wheat. Mix well to coat puffed wheat. Roll into balls or press into buttered 9x13-inch pan. Once cooled, cut into squares.

Date Square/Matrimonial Cake

³/₄ c butter
1 c brown sugar
½ tsp nutmeg
Milk

1 tsp baking soda
1½ c oatmeal
1½ c flour

DATE FILLING:

2 c dates, chopped
½ c brown sugar
1 c warm water

A little lemon juice
   to taste, if
   desired, for more
   flavor

Rub butter into dry ingredients. Add enough milk to hold together. Reserve ½ cup crumbs. Pack the remainder in 8x8-inch cake pan, spread with the date filling, top with the reserve crumbs, and bake at 325–350° for 25–35 minutes.

Nanaimo Bars

BASE:

½ c butter
¼ c sugar
1 egg, beaten
4 tbsp cocoa

2 c graham wafer crumbs
½ c coconut
1 c nuts, chopped

Mix first 4 ingredients in a saucepan and cook until smooth. Add remaining ingredients, mix, and press into 8x8-inch pan. Bake at 350° for 10 minutes or until slightly golden. Cool.

MIDDLE LAYER:

¼ c butter
2 tbsp custard powder

3 tbsp milk
2 c icing sugar

Beat until smooth and spread on top of cooled base.

TOP LAYER:

4 squares semisweet chocolate   1 tsp butter

Melt together and pour on top.

Magic Cookie Bars

½ c margarine or butter
1½ c graham cracker
  crumbs
1 (14-oz) can sweetened
  condensed milk (not evaporated)

1 (6-oz) pkg semisweet
  chocolate chips
1⅓ c flaked coconut
1 c nuts, chopped

Preheat oven to 350° or 325° for glass dish. In 9x13-inch baking pan, melt margarine in oven. Sprinkle crumbs over margarine, mix together, and press into pan. Pour condensed milk evenly over crumbs. Top evenly with remaining ingredients. Press down firmly. Bake 25–30 minutes or until lightly browned. Cool thoroughly before cutting.

Tarts

*"If you come with us,
we will share with you
whatever good things the LORD gives us."*

NUMBERS 10:32

Lemon Tart

2 c sugar
¼ lb butter
Tart shells, baked

2 lemons, rind and juice
4 eggs

Melt butter and sugar in double boiler. Add rind, then beaten eggs and lemon juice. Boil to thicken. Place in baked tart shells. Cool.

Coconut Tarts

1 egg
½ c sugar
Pinch salt
Tart shells, unbaked

1 tbsp butter
1½ c coconut
2 tbsp strawberry jam

Melt butter; add egg and beat well. Add sugar and pinch salt. Blend well. Mix in coconut. Put a drop of jam into each pastry shell; top with a spoon of above mixture. Bake at 350° for 15–20 minutes or until golden brown.

Crab Tarts

Tart shells, unbaked
4 eggs
2 c cream
1/3 c minced onion
1 tsp salt
Dash cayenne pepper

1 can crabmeat, drain and
    pat dry with a paper towel
1 c shredded Swiss or
    mozzarella cheese
Dried parsley flakes, to taste

Beat eggs until blended; stir in cream. Add onion, salt, and pepper. Set aside.

Sprinkle crabmeat and cheese into the tart shells. Pour egg mixture on top. Sprinkle with parsley. Bake at 375° until knife inserted comes out clean, approximately 15–20 minutes.

Vegetables

*Better a meal of vegetables
where there is love
than a fattened calf with hatred.*

PROVERBS 15:17

Hot Artichoke Spread

1 can artichokes, chopped
1 can green chiles, chopped
1 tomato, chopped

¾ c Parmesan, reserve
¼ c for top
1 c mayonnaise

Combine all ingredients. Bake in oven 350° for 20 minutes, or microwave on high for 4–5 minutes.

Crispy Zucchini Strips

3 zucchini
⅓ c flour
1 egg
1 tbsp water

½ c cornflake crumbs
½ tsp seasoned salt
¼ c vegetable oil
¼ c butter

Remove tips from zucchini but do not peel. Cut lengthwise into eighths. Cut each strip in half. Coat strips with flour. In shallow dish, beat together egg and water. In separate shallow dish, combine cornflake crumbs and seasoned salt. Dip each strip into egg wash then into seasoned crumbs, coating evenly.

In large skillet, heat half the oil and butter. Add half the zucchini strips and fry for 4–5 minutes, turning as needed to brown evenly. Remove strips to warm oven (200°). Cook remaining strips in remaining oil and butter.

Vegetable Pizza

Pillsbury croissant dough

Press into ungreased pizza pan and pinch sections together. Brown in 350° oven and cool thoroughly.

MIX:

1 (8-oz) pkg cream cheese
1/2 c mayonnaise
Vegetables

Dash garlic powder
Dill weed, to taste

Top with shredded or nicely broken-up cauliflower, broccoli, carrots, and onions. Top with mozzarella cheese.

Miscellaneous

*Command them to do good,
to be rich in good deeds,
and to be generous and willing to share.*

1 TIMOTHY 6:18

Nuts and Bolts

2 c Cheerios
2 c Crispix
2 c Shreddies
2 c pretzels

4–5 tbsp butter or margarine
2 tsp Worcestershire sauce
1½ tsp onion powder
1½ tsp garlic or seasoning
salt

Melt butter or margarine. Add Worcestershire sauce and spices. Combine all other ingredients in large microwave-safe dish. Add melted mixture and stir well. Microwave on high 4–5 minutes, stirring twice. Cool.

Cheese Chips

½ tsp salt
¼ tsp paprika
1½ c flour
A few grains cayenne
½ c shortening

¾ c grated cheese
Cold water
Milk
Poppy or celery seeds

Combine dry ingredients; cut in shortening. Add cheese. Add enough water to hold ingredients together. Form in roll 1½ inches in diameter. Wrap in waxed paper and chill in refrigerator overnight. Slice thinly. Brush tops with milk and sprinkle with poppy or celery seeds. Bake at 400° until golden; time depends on amount of water used.

Gingerbread for Houses

⅓ c soft shortening
1 c brown sugar, packed
1½ c molasses
⅔ c cold water
1 tsp vanilla
7 c all-purpose flour,
    sifted

2 tsp soda
1 tsp salt
1½ tsp ginger
1 tsp cloves
1 tsp cinnamon
¼ tsp allspice
¼ tsp nutmeg

Combine shortening, sugar, and molasses, and beat until well blended. Stir in water and vanilla. Sift flour, soda, salt, and spices together into mixture and blend thoroughly. Chill several hours or overnight.

Roll and cook on a baking sheet at 350° for 8–10 minutes. When completely cool, construct into Gingerbread House, holding it together with Decorative Icing.

DECORATIVE ICING:

3 egg whites
¼ tsp cream of tartar

1 c icing sugar, sifted

Beat egg whites and cream of tartar until frothy. Add sugar gradually, beating well after each addition. Continue beating until very stiff and glossy. If it begins to get too soft when you are working with it, beat it again with mixer at high speed until firm.

Cheesy Grapes

4 oz cream cheese
$^{1}/_{4}$ c crumbled blue cheese
1 tbsp mayonnaise (approx)
1 clove minced garlic
   (optional)

$^{1}/_{4}$ tsp ground ginger
60 small, firm seedless
   grapes
2 c ground almonds,
   toasted

(To toast almonds, bake on baking sheet at 350° for 5 minutes or until golden.)

In bowl, cream together cheeses and mayonnaise, adding up to 1 tablespoon more mayonnaise for spreading consistency. Stir in garlic, if using, and ginger. Wash grapes and dry on paper towels. Stir grapes into cheese mixture, stirring gently to coat each grape thoroughly, rolling by hand if necessary to completely cover each grape. Roll cheese-covered grapes individually in almonds until coated. Place on flat platter or tray. Cover with plastic wrap and refrigerate for about 1 hour or up to 3 days. Makes 60.

Cheese Straws

½ tsp salt
½ tsp powdered ginger
1 c flour
1 c shredded sharp cheddar
    cheese, about 4 oz

⅓ c butter or margarine
¼ c sesame seed, toasted
½ tsp Worcestershire sauce
2–2½ tsp cold water

Mix salt, ginger, and flour. Cut in butter with a pastry blender. Lightly stir in cheese and sesame seed. Mix Worcestershire sauce with 1 tablespoon of the water and sprinkle over flour; toss with a fork. Add remaining water while tossing, until moistened. Gather up with fingers to form a ball. On a lightly floured board, roll to ⅛-inch thick. Cut with a pastry wheel or knife into strips about 3 inches long and ½-inch wide. Place about 1 inch apart on ungreased baking sheets and bake, uncovered, at 400° for 10–12 minutes, or until lightly browned and crisp. Makes 6–7 dozen.

Cheese Crispies

½ c soft butter
1 c finely grated cheddar
    cheese

1 c flour
Pinch of cayenne
1 c crisp rice cereal

Cream butter and cheese together in medium bowl. Stir in flour, cayenne, and cereal. Mix well. Shape into 1-inch balls. Place on ungreased baking sheets. Flatten with fork. Bake at 375° for 10–15 minutes until golden. They will be more crispy if they are pressed thin. Makes approximately 3 dozen.

Chocolate-Peppermint Pretzels

1 c powdered sugar
½ c butter, softened
½ c shortening
1 egg
1½ tsp vanilla

2½ c flour
½ c cocoa
1 tsp salt
¼ c crushed candy canes

CHOCOLATE COATING:

2 squares unsweetened chocolate
2 tbsp butter

2 c powdered sugar
3–4 tbsp water

FOR COATING:

Melt chocolate and butter; remove from heat. Beat in sugar and water until smooth.

FOR PRETZELS:

Mix sugar, butter, shortening, egg, and vanilla. Stir in dry ingredients, except candy canes. Knead level tablespoons of dough by hand until it's the right consistency for molding. Roll into pencil-like ropes, about 9 inches long. Twist into pretzel shapes on ungreased baking sheet. Bake in 375° oven until set, about 9 minutes. Let stand 1–2 minutes before removing from baking sheet; cool completely. Dip tops of pretzels into coating and sprinkle with crushed candy canes.

Coconutty Banana Bites

5 firm bananas
2 tbsp lemon juice

1 c vanilla yogurt
2 c flaked coconut,
  toasted

(To toast coconut, bake at 350° for 10 minutes or until light golden brown.)

Cut bananas into bite-sized pieces. Dip in lemon juice and drain off excess. Dip in yogurt, then roll gently in coconut to coat. Serve immediately or refrigerate up to 2 hours before serving. Serve with cocktail toothpicks. Makes approximately 30.

Stuffed Dates

1 pkg dates
1 pkg cheddar cheese

1 pkg bacon

Cut bacon strips in half. Fry bacon until halfway cooked. Drain. Cut cheese into small lengths, to taste. Slit dates and stuff with 1 length of cheese each. Wrap with ½ slice bacon. Broil until the bacon is cooked.

Jell-O Trees

2 (8-serving size) pkgs lime
   Jell-O powder

1 pkg unflavored gelatin
3 c boiling water

Mix gelatin in ¼ cup cold water and let sit for 1 minute. Add Jell-O powder to boiled water; add gelatin mixture and mix until completely dissolved. Spray a baking sheet or large cake pan with cooking spray to prevent sticking. When mixture has cooled to room temperature, pour into pan and refrigerate until firm, at least 3 hours. Using Christmas tree-shaped cookie cutters, cut into shapes.

Easy Onion Chip Dip

1 pkg onion soup mix

1 container sour cream

Mix well; serve with plain or rippled chips.

Worship the LORD
your God,
and his blessing will be
on your food and water.

EXODUS 23:25